The Space Carved by the Sharpness of Your Absence

By

Nancy Murphy

12/2022

To making "space" for poetry!

Nancy Murphy

Gyroscope Press

Gyroscope Press
PO Box 1989
Gillette, WY 82717
gyroscopepress@gmail.com

The Space Carved by the Sharpness of Your Absence
Copyright © 2022 by Nancy Murphy
First Edition 2022

Cover photo by: Kim Emerson
Author Photo by Schlick Art
Cover Design, Interior Layout by Constance Brewer
© 2022

ISBN: 978-1-7367820-3-3

Published in the United States of America

Table of Contents

for Mom, your passing my heartbreak
for Monica, your arrival my heart salve

The Space Carved by the Sharpness of Your Absence

What I Want You to Know

I choose to live in the spaces
carved by the sharpness
of your absence.
It's not what you think.
Neglect becomes me, my desire
gathers and elongates so that
if our shoulders should touch
when we walk, you know,
by accident,
the heat in me catches
like a burner. And you can see
a small opening between
my lips where steam escapes.

Field of View
  after painting by Andrew Wyeth, "Christina's World"

I am a stretched canvas. My mother's
yearning background color. Dress dusty

pink the color of my first ballet slippers,
hair putting up a fight. Thin black belt around

my nickel of a waist, it takes me years
to become a body. A girl even longer.

The field is everything to me. The way sunlight
wakes up the colors, the way the hint

of a road slices space into before
and after, the way home keeps moving

away. Collapsing onto the grass,
oblivious to how it can stain you,

mark you as a child. When do we start
seeing the world as wider than we can

hold? I paint myself away from the edges
of the picture, on another coast, different

weather. I paint the story of my mother
and what she wanted. I remember when

she gazed on me, and when she gazed not
on me. I carry hollowness into the rain.

How Isolation is Like Summer

Remember the slow heaviness of August
in Albany,
the 60s, sixth grade
everything exhausting
from humidity,
excessive greenery suffocating,
days   stretching   in our hands like
the wonder of boardwalk
taffy that never breaks, it gets thinner
and thinner   and thinner.
Remember when effort was pointless,
when summer kept us
low to the ground, sitting in the art
of doing nothing, tree filtered sunlight
moving across our freckled faces
as we spoke
quietly, like whispers might keep us
cooler.
Picture us young, self-contained, still
whole. Breathing the not knowing
of life like
it was our daily bread.

Where did my blue paisley shirt
go, the one that would get translucent
with sweat. Mom, I can't find it.
Where did it go?

Where did you go?

Oh the trouble with looking
for things, what you find.
This impossible brokenness of
motherlessness,
how that grief lies in wait for you,
coiled, attacks only in self

defense, no one wants
to be forgotten. Memory
is a mother.

Lipstick

I miss lipstick, that mark of power,
bright outlining of mouth like scandal,
names like seduction: rouge, nude,
plum, caramel. Now lipstick only
creates blistering rebellion, too many
years of red dye. Just when I could use one,
lips faded to the color of freckles
on a face aged to a blur.
                        When I was new to all this, working
in an office in the sky
in a city of oily trains, bright
blue glass, heels stepping carefully
around sidewalk grates, I applied
lipstick every morning, *applied*
meaning tried, meaning wanted
them to see me. Work was a world
of men—suits, shiny leather, sleek
briefcases, endless algorithms
of blue, gray and stripe. I understood
the rules. I liked the rules. I thought
the rules would protect me. My skirted
suits the length and tightness
to reveal me female but not secretary,
brightly colored paisleys around
my neck (easily untied).
                        Soon I would discover the office
was bursting with indiscretions,
invisible to me through the haze
of our after-hours drinking. I thought
it was only me misbehaving, staring
across the floor at him longer
than is incidental, feeling that series
of small clicks when we first talked,

a locksmith shifting a dial,

making my insides tumble.
          Now I know that such things are only
a game, like roulette, the one with the loaded
gun. Back then I thought they meant
more, that they couldn't be ignored,
that what followed was sacred. I never
imagined this could be habit forming.

This is How it Works
after Kelly Cressio-Moeller, "A Night of One's Own"

Every time is a first for something, a first second even.

I remember how the trees bowed to me. They emerged
    from the fog that morning like saints.

Nature doesn't defend itself when you yell at it. Like it doesn't
    care.

What makes me calm, what I won't tell you.

Blood on paper looks like ketchup, like you were just eating
    your dinner when it happened.

I could stand if I had to. I could drive us too, if I had to.

Candles start things, fires, kisses. Light bouncing, you forget
    yourself.

Some things can only be written in invisible ink, on the inside
    of your eyelids.

I want to change one thing about myself, but I had my chance.

A still life is another way to die.

There's an orbit here and it's not around me. It never was.

I'm not leaving this party crying.

Love and Death in November

November makes sense as a month for death,
nature is headed that way anyway, the gravitas

hard to resist. My mother didn't say
goodbye to anyone, and I don't remember now

the last words we spoke on the phone, miles
apart. She heard my newborn daughter's cries

through the wires, never saw her face,
its perfection and beauty unsurpassed by any

child ever born in the history of the world.
They are all the same, children, in that distinction,

my mother would have known that. I am bereft
of that single gaze, my mother upon my child.

To be witnessed in my transformation
from daughter to mother, the very thing

that bound us. It burns in me, this love
and loss. Now my girl grown and gone,

to live the same miles away from me.
Maybe she senses my bottomless longing,

protects her life from me. Or maybe it's just
the natural order, this painful rupture

of child from parent. I remember.
She reaches out when it suits her like a cruel

ex-lover who sometimes misses you and calls,
knowing that you will always love them,

that being needed is a gift they are bestowing.
How being her mother makes me feel

like I am my mother, and how feeling
like my mother brings her alive again,

fixes the broken part of our circle, a circle
that keeps coming around again. Every November.

airport, night flight

like a hospital waiting room, airport departure wings are full of
small talk and long silences and what sits underneath. I see
parents sit on either side of me at the gate in
philadelphia, back when you could do that kind of thing
I always protested,
they always insisted.

now I follow my sandy blonde college girl around
bradley international terminal, clinging to the
seconds before she succumbs to security,
asking questions that don't matter with urgency
do you have something to read?
she raises her hand to stop me, blinks affirmatively.

we've already said as much as could be said,
considering. she is the age when I started to
know myself. I remember so well I think
she is me, when she lets me into her worries
I remember too well: we share the same nervous system,
I feel her burdens like they are my own.
mostly I am relieved she trusts me again,
redeemed after the silent years, the secret
years, the scary years.

north gate now, I let her release me first from
our embrace, our parting words stumble out jaggedly-

Whatagreatvisitgoodluckyeahitwasmomwitheverythingimso
Proudofyouthankyoucallmewhenyouiwilliwillarrive

—then I watch as she moves forward into the jaws
of the larger world, she doesn't turn back
until the last second, knows I wait for this
final crumb—the one who leaves has all the power—
she raises her hand, birdlike, and smiles without showing

teeth. Then her eyes dance when I play my part
as the pursuing suitor waving with all of me.
I watch the hem of her trench coat follow her
around the corner.

Father (Mother)

My father's hearing is starting to go.
He chooses to miss things, refuses an aid,
doesn't catch the 2 a.m. phone
call. I am the one who tells him

five hours later, Lee passed in the night.
I am the one who absorbs his shock
and sob. I thought he was prepared
but bad news is like that. She is the second

wife he has survived, the first my mother
twenty-five years ago. When I arrive
at his door that day, we make our usual
resemblance of an embrace, his eighty-eight

year old frame bent into a C, keeping
his heart from me. We sit side by side on the sofa,
the vintage flowered wallpaper suddenly
alive as if communing with Lee's wild
garden outside the front window, the roses

bloom that week. I rub his bony back like
he is my child. The only other time I saw
him cry, at LAX arrivals,

my daughter three weeks old, my mother
two weeks gone. Me seeing him, him seeing
her, all that living and dying, all that
unreasonable pain.

I missed my mother's funeral, too soon
after birth to fly. My father tells me he is the same
sad now as then and I feel betrayed. My parents
married forty-one years, isn't time how you
measure grief? He writes a eulogy
for Lee, then falters. I agree

to stand in for him. He depends on me
that way. I take him to doctor appointments,
repeat orders. He does what he likes, ignores

the rule about salt, declines a daily walk.
We know he won't live forever, but jesus
he has to try. He returns east, lives with
my brother in the old house. Everyone else

helps. Some days I feel like seaweed
come loose from the ocean floor, unmoored,
drifting away until you can't see me.

I am no longer the mother.
No one is the mother now.

All that Bergamot*

We are on our way from LA to Zion,
the one in Utah. We stop in Hemet,

the desert, a Starbucks. I need a midday
lift. A man sits in a battered wheelchair

by the entrance, no hat. It's 102 degrees.
His clothes an assembly of fabrics

the color of an espresso he can't afford.
Sunburnt leathered face, patches

of a beard, he was a blonde once. He was
a lot of things once. I motion Brian

to avoid walking past him. It's just
a reflex. Not personal. Inside the cool

café I order my usual—tea latte
with English Breakfast tea, *not*

Earl Grey (all that bergamot!),
soy milk for its sweet vanilla traces,

one Splenda, something I hope
doesn't kill me one day if they find

it causes cancer. I've tried to quit
and I just can't. As I wait I notice

how I'm still able to make eye contact
with strangers even with our masks on.

I think—we are all learning to use
our eyes more. Humans are a wonder.

The man outside the door comes into mind.
No one looks him in the eye. Sympathy floods

me, and some shame. But what does that buy?
Even so, I resolve to give him something,

and to ask him something. I say nothing
as we exit. He turns towards us, the usual

beginning, *Hey do you….*I lurch forward,
drop some bills into his lap so I don't

have to touch his hands, because, well
covid of course. Then I pause, lean in, take in

his face. I say, *What's your name?*
He startles, squints, replies, *What's my name?*

I turn quickly now with a small wave,
mumble goodbye, hurry on to the car,

flushed from the heat, the moment.
Brian stands waiting, holding my door

open for me, a habit he can't break,
a habit that makes me impatient. I'm

ungrateful like that.   Then I hear
a voice calling out behind me.

Floyd. My name is Floyd.

* The characteristic flavor of Earl Grey tea
comes from the addition of bergamot.

Betty, Poolside

She pleads with him to join her
in the water, at first lightly,
then with a rising insistence.
He resists. She is unhappy.
It is always the same, the woman
calling the man to her, wanting
to float together in their skin,
and he on the edge of falling,
regaining footing, then diving in
when she is not looking. He is
on his own time. Betty's beauty
strikes me and I wonder if he sees it
anymore the way the world does,
how any other man could not
say no. I learn they are married
one year now. She talks to me
in the Jacuzzi. I tell her
I left my husband because
he would not swim naked with me
in the dark in the pool behind
the fence at our house.

Devil's Holiday
   after poet Nadia Tuéni

Of course it lives in you, you put it under the pillow
yourself. It's 4 am again, breathing will only take you

so far. Of course any rain would be welcome, but
too much is a kind of regret. Of course love is a blushing

mimosa tree when it's in bloom, how else can you explain
yourself? Of course marriage is sacred, like earth,

like diamonds. Of course desire is the devil's holiday,
the way your cool blues swam to his warm chocolate

browns, irresistible you say later. Of course death
is a spider weaving the only thing it knows. The threads

never break but it's messy. They stick to you and you
will do anything to get away from them. Jump

in the river, drink all the wine. Of course you see
what you're doing. Of course you can stop.

Of course you don't.

Dahlias

One summer she feels only grief.

Another summer she sees
dahlias for the first time,

their long stems leaning, almost
failing

to hold up plump pink
and crimson blooms.
Wonders whether
it's said day-lias or dahhh-lias,
or if it depends on where you're from.
Everything of course depends
on where you're from,
what you did,
who knows.
We all sin. Sometimes not

even originally. Mid-life flirtations
with young men
lead to compromises,
conversations
about technicalities.

It all started when she found her first
gray hair   there.
She chased rapture,
believed she was closing in on it.
Couldn't turn back. Wouldn't.
After, nothing looked

the same. The way he flossed—
how her skin crawled—
you can't ignore these things.
This is the life she made.

And she made it that dahlia
summer, failing
to resist.

Fluency

I am going to learn Spanish before I go
to Madrid. By learn I mean re-learn. When
I was younger, I knew things that I have since
forgotten, not because I'm old but because
there are so many time zones to learn. I thought
I knew where this story was going, but I haven't
decided yet where I want it to go. For one thing,
men confused me. Their want of me scented
with vanilla and mint or orange blossoms,
sometimes the sea. I hungered too. Remember
the lavender blooms along the road between
our hotel and that village. Parfait. My favorite
French word, you had so many more.
The English are like that, hating the French
but spending all their time and money there.
They learn to speak it passably, as they say. Possibly.
The guilt of leaving you burns not without a little
pleasure. I am alive and well and living I want to say.
I am sorry, I think. Sorry to write back with no
ambivalence, there is no subtext between
us anymore. The one I am with is the one
I am with. We are all so flawed, moving
from one person to the other just raises hope.

Dimming

Let me tell you about leaving,
how it was almost
easy. Sometimes a mandarin
is so ripe that its skin wants
to be peeled, falls away
as your fingers get close,
pockets of air under the surface

waiting for release. I was ready
like that, open to other
hands, mouths, scents.
I feared being skipped over,
not picked in time. Frostbite.
At first it was a long December
then it was spring

in my step, everyone noticed.
Still I buried a guilt that
I could have done better,
that I had no right
to ripen. I had a secret
tally of faults that I used
against myself like a rainstorm.
I made judges out of accidental
men, took punishment
hungrily. Until

it was enough. Only then
could I let myself look
back, see how smugly
we walked the streets
of Philadelphia, rapt,
wrapped around each other.
Then baby daughter
mornings in the corner
condo, LA beach sun

streaming in, smells
of talcum. Remember,
I said almost. We were once
a light, he and I.
What did we know
then of dimming?

Dreaming

It always starts the same,   we are somewhere.
Last night
it was a dinner, someone's house.
I hadn't seen you
in years. You looked like
the last time I saw you, boyish
chest had started to barrel,   waist with a hint
of an impending thickening,
you can't be impossibly
what you were   forever.

It always feels the same,
that pull to you
like a welcome death,
a blessing in the shape of a pulse,
our own gravity.
We let it heavy us,
the casual bumping of limbs,
deeper warmth.
We seek a place to hunger,   a balcony
in the open but out of earshot, arouse
no one.
We are always   watched,
always   afraid of being seen.
Your hand on the small
of my back,   barely.

I awake
covered in a honeyed urgency,
forgetting again how skinned I felt
when you left.
I gather the bedding around me, try to contain
the ether of last night
only to feel it seep out,   float   up
to a morning mackerel sky.

Sometimes a Wild Saint
after Tom Hiron, "Sometimes a Wild God"

Sometimes a wild saint will storm in while
you're at the stove
searing steaks,
tapping smoked paprika
onto sweet potatoes. She'll start

a fire in the blue room, open the best

Burgundy   without asking,
crank up

the Stones. Sometimes a wild saint
is not exactly
drunk, (but not undrunk)

maybe beyond

drunk like I was
in my twenties after work

in bars with married co-workers.
I'm not here to confess,   I'll just say

I have seen how things can break

down, how anything can be
forgiven, how miracles are   not
that rare   really.

Sometimes a wild saint

is such a martyr, deadly
serious.   But I'm not

going to fall
into that deep

well of belief again, the longing
that follows, all that embarrassment
when god doesn't show up
in time.

Sometimes a wild saint
will remind us that there will be summer

again, that I will be able to go underwater
and feel cool on my entire head
and not even care
if my hair   ever
dries.

Heat and Other Burnings

I love the way the body burns
within from forward motion
in winter. In Dublin I watch a young
girl weaving around slow walkers,
jumping across narrow streets
as buses bear down. Stepping
into a basement coffeehouse,
she sheds her heavy coat
and woolen scarf wrapped
around her wet mouth
and innocence. And her heat

and secrets release into the room
all at once, the smell a mix
of sweat,
sandalwood
and recklessness.

                        A girl tries to keep her secrets close,
          they are the mistakes she yearns to make.
               A woman knows the currency
                           of confession,
            what it can buy, how you pay, how it
                             frees you.

She is on the left side of
virginity, itching to
cross a line, soon to be
awakened, well
soon to act like she is
awake. It isn't a lie
exactly. I want to tell her
it takes a woman
a lifetime to know
if she is real or only appears so
in a mirror. The reflection is skin

deep, cool as glass. Look into
the eyes. Sadness first lands there,
then the jaw, the line of the lips.

Aftermath

After my mother died, I left my husband.
He had always been a rock

but I stumbled upon someone more
like fire, and I needed to ignite,

breathe into the blue edge of a flame,
find myself in what remained.
.
Friday night I slice into red peppers,
he scorches them on the grill

along with sweet corn, chicken in dried
thyme. Together ten years now

and I still call him new, this is just how
I talk, tell myself I'm free, remind

myself that I could be reduced to ashes
again. Only burning can purge this longing

for all that's lost, for all that's found,
for those careless nights and all that blazed.

It's a long way

from Cahersiveen to Galway. We start in the morning,
head north. I read him directions from my phone

as he shifts the gears of the tiny red Renault. How smooth
the ride feels considering how he handles an automatic.

I speak clearly and slowly, and with an Irish accent
for no reason except that it feels truer. Sometimes

he hears me, makes the correct turn, other times
he doesn't hear me because he's thinking. This difference

between us a constant. I understand it. (I don't like it.)
Fog slips in, spills out over tops of shaggy hedges,

moves in and out of forests like the quietest army. Gray skies
reflected in the lakes & bays & estuaries & ocean we pass.

Then drizzle. Wipers on and off, uneven this rain and not
rain-ness. Our first night the soft swoosh of showers lulled us

to sleep. Waking in a fog a few hours later, strange half
dreaming, jet lag I suppose. It's been like that this week.

Cloudy with bright cerulean patches and blinding sun,
minutes later a multitude of black swirls, some touching

the water with a frizzle of rain. Their darkness screams across
the bay towards us as we run back to the car. The wind too,

punishing at the sharp cliffs, then a quiet break. We need to
be here, to remember what keeps us together, to spend hours

in a car where the silence slices both ways. As we continue,
we find a seventh century church on an unplanned (lost again)

route, a welcome hot tea cart at a chilly beach, plump oysters
just plucked from the stony sea. And always the comfort

of the green—on the emerald pastures we whip past,
on the mossy stone walls that chase us along the narrow

byways, and on the tall trees that gather and reach over us,
hold us in a verdant tunnel of their making. We feel

a blessing as we pass under. We carry it with us.
Late now, but still   light in this far north summer.

Anniversary

Irish rain chases us around January, climbs
into our bodies seeking warmth.
Instead of romantic evenings,
we split packs of cough drops, turn
away in the dark; the space between us
thickens with my disappointment, gives me
reason to hold back.

We push forward on this road trip,
Connemara maroon hills bleed
into bright green fields, blue-black
north Atlantic waves. Wildflowers
find footing in forgotten soil.
There is resistance in this land,
survival, a refusal to surrender.

We stop in an ancient village, hold
hands, share a pot of tea. He pours
the milk in, then the tea. He makes mine
first every time. It's unfair how he does that.
The silence between us softens,
almost like forgiveness.

Petrified

Pink dust collects
on our shoes as we tackle
the Taos trail.   The faces

of the rocks are wrinkled,
lined with stories of upheaval and
erosion.
It happened slowly, millions
of years, but
it is no less violent to be
shattered that way than

quickly.
I am losing
my footing
and sliding as we walk
back down the hill, shaky with
fatigue, thirst. Water

is the creator and
destroyer of rocks,
insinuating itself into small veins
until they broke apart.
Here too minerals invaded drowning
trees, trapped in rivers,
airless,
until they became stone,

petrified.   I am afraid
of invasion,
of loss to you, loss of you.
How easy it is for some
forces to push through,
wear down. After the hike,
our bodies are open, warm to
the touch. Cloudbursts erupt
around us, between us,
between legs, between cries.

I Don't Mind Cooking (Every Night)

I decide at breakfast that dinner
will be stir-fried in the wok.
There are always ripening

things that must be eaten
by today. He heads to the garden
with usual purpose. I clean

a patio chair, brush my teeth, check
for mail again. How long a day can be!
When the clock finally climbs

into dusk, I switch on the overhead
lights in the blue and white tiled kitchen
and search for music. Patty Griffin

wails about the long way home.
Her vibrato reaches down
my throat and I am dry and alone.

I take out chicken to bring it to room
temperature before cooking,
I read that was important. I imagine

the chill that is setting in tonight even though
it hit 81 here in LA. I squander
this easy life, I could have had a summer

afternoon. Instead I stayed inside,
as if it were early winter like where
I am from. I want to be where

I used to be again. I don't want to
move though. So many boxes.
I can change my mind in a shorter

distance than the length of a real
winter. Some days there is so much
cutting. I waste most of the asparagus.

I like things trimmed. A massage therapist
told me my left arm hurts because of fear-
holding tight, holding back.

What about the heavy pots I asked?
I add quinoa to boiling water, set
a timer because I will forget. I would skip

grains but he won't feel full. He might be
lonely too, I'm not good at this
close living. Some days I would rather

not be looked at for example. And I truly
forget to be thankful. Where is the timer
for that? I wonder if Tuesday

is too soon for white wine. Broccoli
tumbles until it turns the most cheerful
green, a little Christmas in a pan

with dancing red peppers. I plate
our two dinners, add a sprinkle of white
sesame seeds, something I saw in a recipe.

It looks fancy. He wraps a band-aid
around my finger, another cut
from the new knife. It takes two hands.

Winter's White

after Louise Glück, "Early December in Croton-on-Hudson"

Ice is wider than water, dwarfs the shoreline.
Where is the river now? How the water moves
under the surface, slides away from you when
you notice it. When someone you want
feels your reaching, lets that flood them, then   ice.

Bone white we say, a color to choose
for a wall. As if we know, as if we can see into the center
of each other, as if we know the difference between
stone colored bone and ice.

The quiet that snow sends out when you stand
still.   Not unlike isolation,
when you meet your own eyes in the mirror.
You were just combing your hair, then a buckling,
the weight of what you miss. Outside,
icicles in sunlight melting, dripping.

Overhead, a black bird circles. I will always want
some you. The pulse of that keeps me
alive like a steady tap on my shoulder, someone
keeping me awake when I'm driving
at night,   you never see black ice.

Manual for Handling a Catastrophe During a Pandemic

First, don't exaggerate. You are not the first person
to get bad news. His heart needed repair, it had to be
opened. This is not a love poem.

Second, when he gets home from the hospital, drive
to CVS every day for nine days. Hold your breath
when you're inside so you don't get Covid and bring it
home because if he gets that, you can stop reading right

now. Third, or is it fifth, make a post-it note that says
good morning and draw a smiley face with curly hair.

Sixth, put it next to a white coffee cup, the kind
that usually goes with a saucer, which is a shape no one
uses for coffee anymore. It's like coffee in the '50s
in your kitchen with a neighbor. Seventh, there are no

neighbors now. We can't talk to anyone outside
our immediate house. Unless they're daughters. But they
can't be here either.

Twelfth night. Anyway, the coffee cup is for the handful
of pink and white pills he has to take. Write that down.

Fourth, sorry, define catastrophe. If you listen in the night
for proof of life, it's a catastrophe. If you see
him from the hallway asleep in the chair where he was
bravely watching TV in the afternoon and it suddenly
makes you weep, it's a catastrophe.

Fifth, don't tell everyone. It's boring. It makes you boring.
It makes you like everyone else. Besides everyone else has
their own pandemic catastrophe and I am not a good listener.

Sixth, don't forget to bathe once in a while, but don't bother
to wash your hair, it always looks the same clean or dirty.
Seventh, no one is looking at you.

Tenth, don't hesitate to call. Hesitate to call. No one
can help you anyway. Think of a friend or maybe a sister
you can cry to on the phone, but you won't have time for that.

Eighth, don't think about the time before the catastrophe.
Don't remember that you two were doing pretty well
          considering.
Ninth, think about the day he handed you
a piece of paper with the diagnosis.

Fifteenth, the paper was a map of our lives for the next
six months. What it didn't say is if we would survive.

Third, have some fun with this! Think of as many words
as you can using the letters that spell C a r e t a k e r.

Taken   carefully
taking in   taking on   water
waiting to be taken
cared   couldn't care   wanted to not care
carefully taking off   clothes
even socks
slow down

Eighteenth,   be careful there
careless   carelessly taking care

Nineteenth, afraid to care
afraid to stop caring
afraid to stop
afraid to

Twentieth,   be afraid.

A Piece of the Calm
after Mark Strand, "A Piece of the Storm"

From the California sky, silver sun slides into the kitchen
between the slats in the window shades. It doesn't wait for me
to notice, it is beyond needing things like that from this world.
It taps on the table, not impatiently. I am reading the news
of the day, weeping, sipping breakfast tea from the other side
of the world, English tea is really from Assam, Kenya, Ceylon,
Darjeeling. How I miss the mystery of the old names.
Sunlight tiptoes closer, I have that feeling when someone is
watching you, and I look up from what has pulled me down.
One thing leads to another, I watch how the fuzzy headed treetops
out the back window waltz with the glimmering
from above, I listen as the doves flutter their adoration
for each other.   I pour from the half-full teapot.

How to Drive Off a Cliff

As you climb the mountainside hugging
the unguarded road, you imagine the worst.
You push on because there is an empty beach
between two rocks calling from the other
side and you want to be alone. You want to feel
honeyed sun on the top of your head as you
watch waves tap out messages on the sand.
You want to break the code. As the car
accelerates, your hands search the stitching
along the wheel, you notice the soft spots,
recall all the miles this body has taken you.
The wine colored mountains your eyes
follow on the horizon recede as you miss
the last turn and start the somersault down.
Nearby sheep graze, one locks eyes with you,
silently asks if there is something you need,
you both know it is too late. You nod
back in gratitude to the animal and let go like
you have just arranged that last pillow before
sleep. In your mouth, a familiar bittersweet,
not unlike that last sip from your morning teacup,
a mix of milk and leaves and debris at the bottom.

After Life

On the way to where I am going
I pray that I will be taken along

a corniche just south of Grasse in Provence,
where coming around a turn, a bloom

of magenta bougainvillea barely
hides a slice of the Mediterranean–

sapphire, like the color of the ring
I lost while pushing crumbs out

of the back seat after taking my small
daughter out of the car. He'd surprised

me with this rare gift while we waited
for her to arrive.   After this life,

I would find that ring and wear it
again, not in apology just proof of something

that mattered. I would also discover
my mother's diamond, and remember

the way it broke free of its setting after so
many years intact, the way I have never been

the same since she left here early, the way
I loved hugging this circle of her around me.

Other things have been lost,
like hope   and my favorite black

bra (divorce), and if I have to lose
this life to find all of them, well

at least there is some consolation.
That and an eternal view of the sea

while sipping Montrachet and eating
oysters, the smell of some celestial

lilac in the air like in my childhood
backyard on Myrtle Avenue, a time

when all the rings encircled
me,   fit into each other.

Acknowledgments

Grateful acknowledgment is made to the following journals in which these poems, some in previous versions, first appeared:

Altadena Poetry Review: "airport, night flight"

Aurora Poetry Contest winner: "How Isolation is Like Summer"

The Baltimore Review: "Betty, Poolside"

Blue Heron Review: "A Piece of the Calm"

The Ekphrastic Review: "Field of View"

glassworks: "Anniversary"

Gyroscope Review: "Sometimes a Wild Saint"

Montana Mouthful: "Aftermath"

Sheila-Na-Gig: "How to Drive off a Cliff"

Stoneboat Literary Journal: "Father (Mother)"

SWWIM Every Day: "Dimming"

Thirteenth Moon: "What I Want You to Know," excerpted from "Absence"

Thanks

I would like to thank Constance Brewer, Editor of Gyroscope Press, for her support and steady guidance in selecting my manuscript and then helping bring it to life as this book, my first!

Many thanks to Tresha Faye Haefner and The Poetry Salon, in whose classes many of these poems broke ground and bloomed. The daily offerings were a lifeline during the pandemic and created a great sense of community. Thank you to all my fellow writers there who shared their souls and who offered helpful and encouraging feedback on my work.

A deep thank you to Sarah Maclay and the "Nightbirds" Monday night group, and Hilda Weiss for inviting me in, for critiquing many of the poems in the book. It's such a warm group under Sarah's kind and intelligent guidance. Thank you to Elline Lipkin whose classes last year were instrumental in generating and workshopping some newer work and for helping me further shape my manuscript.

I am so appreciative of all those who hosted the myriad of online classes and readings/open mics over the past couple of years- and for sometimes inviting me to feature- Rick Lupert at Cobalt Cafe, Kai Coggin at Wednesday Night Poetry, Elena Secota's Rapp Saloon Poetry, Peggy Dobreer's Slow Lightning, IWWG readings, and many many others. Through the magic of zoom, poetry flourished and grew beyond its normal boundaries of geography; the connections that arose were numerous and deep.

I want to extend special thanks to my family and close friends who always read what I write and always say they like it. I'm beyond grateful that my Dad is here to share this moment with me! And lastly, thanks to Brian for his constant love and his encouragement to not hold anything back.

About the Author

Nancy Murphy is a Los Angeles based writer and performer and 2020 winner of the *Aurora Poetry* contest. Previous publications include *Gyroscope Review*, *SWWIM Every Day*, *The Baltimore Review*, *The South Carolina Review*, *Stoneboat Literary Journal*, *Sheila-Na-Gig*, *glassworks*, *The Ekphrastic Review*, *Blue Heron Review*, *Louisville Review* and others. She was recently featured in "Poets on Craft" at the online arts magazine *Cultural Daily*.

A long time volunteer at WriteGirl, Nancy has mentored teens through writing programs. In 2016, she wrote and performed a solo show in various venues including the Hollywood Fringe Festival where she earned an Encore Award. Nancy grew up in upstate NY and holds a B.A. in American Studies from Union College, Schenectady, NY. www.nancymurphywriter.com

Gyroscope Press
PO Box 1989
Gillette, WY 82717
gyroscopepress@gmail.com

Made in the USA
Middletown, DE
03 December 2022

16348455R00031